KUROSAWA'S DOG

KUROSAWA'S DOG

Dennis Hinrichsen

Oberlin College Press
Oberlin, Ohio

The FIELD Poetry Series, vol. 23
Oberlin College Press, 50 N. Professor Street, Oberlin, OH 44074

www.oberlin.edu/ocpress

Cover and book design: Steve Farkas

Library of Congress Cataloging-in-Publication Data

Hinrichsen, Dennis.
  Kurosawa's dog / Dennis Hinrichsen.
    p. cm. — (The Field poetry series ; v. 23)
  ISBN-13: 978-0-932440-34-1 (pbk. : alk. paper)
  ISBN-10: 0-932440-34-7 (pbk. : alk. paper)
  I. Title
  PS3558.I546K87 2009
  811'.54—dc22
                              2008042089

Contents

MASTER

(Quote)
The straw dog barks, daybreak.

ANSWER
"Bow-wow" [the pupil barks like a dog].

from *The Sound of the One Hand: 281 Zen Koans
with Answers,* translated by Yoel Hoffman

I

Bresson's Donkey

Au Hasard, Balthazar

I could believe in Jesus if there were an animal
                    to be beaten
          down, all

that bagpipe braying from the gut's
                    spiritual core
          hauling some Boschian tower of hay

down a rutted

road. 1960s maybe, small town France.
                    A black-and-
          white, flat-light,

feel-of-grace for it. The Christ-like howling
                    ricocheting
          through the square as some

dense farmer leathers in the thinnest
                    of switches—
          a velocity that burns—the wrist-flick

pulling it back

as if to say he's sorry. As if that could
                    work. As if
          Gérard were no less evil

for the oil he spills—elsewhere in the film—
                    curve in the road.
          How he turns away

before the crash,

the noise of wreckage is enough. The girl
                    is enough.
          I can't tell who is creature now,

all those sad eyes and silken hair,
                    the slope
          of the back—donkey and woman—given up

to whip and

cock. Sometimes I think Gérard is too beautiful
                    for the gods,
          that the gods,

in fact, have tethered themselves hard fast
                    to some
          rigidity in the darkness

so they can swing

widely by—sails slack—the switchblade
                    sheen
          of his living. The little motor scooter

engine strapped like a bomb
                    to the frame
          of it.

Moor, he sings,

moor and be merry. We can ruin
                    this world
          together. Beat the horse down. Beat

the woman down. The child, the drunk.
There is
beauty in it... If You can eat

through the clay of my heart, I will
have You.
I will surrender

my eyes. Ride mule to Your approximate heaven.

Portrait of My Father as the Heather Vole

Yellow hair, blue eyes: that was the face of the child by the side of the road. As if the empire of corn had deserted him. Jack-knife in his open palm. Weed tips bending. And so he lived at tree line, at the edge of forests, in uphill heaths. His burrow dug out with claw. The dark soil lifted above the tiles in a clodded froth. The Farmall rocking, cradling his father, or one of the hands, like a hail-wrecked blossom. Then summer's drift. The total length of the animal measured in creek water, the turns of branches; the dorsal fur, a grizzled brown; the underbelly, ventral fur: silver, gray. Did not hibernate. But languished in snow. On its very surface. What sustained him: willow bark, birch bark, heath plants, the budding network of stars through the obsidian quarter panes of his window frosting white—the stars' gold spill, arsenic push. Survived seventeen years. His enemies: the combine, ermine, tractor, marten, hammer and hawk.

On a Watch Chain Woven from Hair, Dated 23.10.22

> "[It has] no voice. [It is] nearly paralytic."
> —*Francis Ponge,* "Fauna and Flora"

And yet how easily it is drawn
through the hand,
three braided strands

clipped midpoint
with the husband's
emblematic "N."

A locket at one end.
The wife's portrait:
sepia, cream.

On the
other half-heart,
open hinge: a snarl

of unbraided hair…
Earlier,
the shears

an unforgiving stork
held away
from the scalp.

Something in her mind
moving like water or
minnows: girlhood

and childing,
a new language and
childing, the

shears' silver
blurring in the mirror's
glare... Then

the groomed acres, cattle
and pasture.
Ten thousand nights.

A tin thimble thumbing
needles through
threadbare shirts. Winter:

one long tumor of
chill; summers
like pools of butter.

Or even less than this—
the cut-boned body
of her husband.

Fieldstone at calf
and bicep. Raw meat
of the face; milk

of belly and buttocks.
Up and out
into black dawn

just cutting flame into
day's wood. Her
hair grown

back by then, grayed.
My father
says, my father says…

but what my
father says now is
nothing. She

was from Hamburg.
She had red hair. Her
name was Christine.

The Sound-of-One-Hand-Clapping Shout

Begins in the breath,
in the sweet moisture pulled from the coagulant air, his wife

wetting her finger to turn night's pages.
It could be the sorrow of memory, of marriage and dying—

he's up at 4 AM to aspirate the serum,
to suck down the mystifying drops—driven over tongue and
    larynx,

through voice box—a collapsing *OM*—
into the pockets of his lungs.

It might as well be this: some Jesus whistle, cry of a hawk,
droplets pearling the milkweed pods—

never not existing, never quite existing—sheen
of Buddha's skin, the smell of the tree still on him.

For it is heaven where he settles. Above
the level of the highest clouds, the sky gone wide, volcanic,

Iowa, Kansas.
Down below, the child posing with objects: hay rake

and tractor, pitchfork, dented bucket, the milk
so heavy in the bell of tin it is white lead, molten rock.

And a man there (not God) to take his money
(the milk—still animal warm—wetting

his ankles).
And a woman there to coil her rattlesnake of braids.

The presence of God (not man) in the silos,
in the precious metal spill of corn, in pig snout and butchered
    cattle,

in the thrill of snakeskin
through the cage of his hands like black-diamond chiseled,

living water, reduced to one raw splinter, night or evening,
the blade of a knife. He digs

it out. He breathes it in. Christ's tears. Whitman's mulish
scent. Mohammed's evaporated cry on his night ride to
    Jerusalem.

Cruel All Moons and Bitter the Suns

Arthur Rimbaud, *The Drunken Boat*

My father swims the Wapsipinicon—body of
        a child, body
           of a poet, upon the body of the stream—

Southern Iowan Drift Plain, his white hands,
           white arms,
             the beginnings of a canvas sheet. In another

zone, another wash, talus slope—the cannibal
           histories:
            the collared lemming, remnant

skull-work, the heather or mountain vole,
           layered as the current
        is layered,

twisting through the hillsides. Still he floats. An animal
           presence—
           a herd of cattle—companion field—

lies down in his lungs. Pressure of rib and
           water and
            longing and breath and grass. The waters let him

go his own free way. There is a wing
           in the shadow of
            evening, a black wind in his hands that fashions

a bleached-white bone. Dutch Creek fissure, washout,
        Empty Fissure
    nearly devoid of sediment

though there is something dark, dense, organic-rich—
        a light, orangish-red silt
    that appears to be *in situ.*

Sound of his singing beneath the torn up sky.
        Daylight fading,
    a colony of doves;

star-infused, bleeding Sea.
        He wants to show his mother a gold fin
    hanging in a blue wave,

a flower he can shake through the barn in a tremble
        of pollen,
    twig bark so waterlogged

it peels off in chunks. Sheath of the water flensed
        from the sheath
    of wood, like a snake's slow kiss into

cooling moistness… decaying body
        of a swan.
    "O countless golden birds, O Force to come"—

he's out of the water now, running, his pants
        hitched high:
    class amphibian, *dirty child.*

At the doorway, gilded threshold, his mother's
        flesh recoils—
    class reptilian, fragment of shell.

He puts his head down into the hearth's lap. It is
                    late, it is
            evening. He watches firedogs flicker,

flake… What he loves best: slurs
                    of runoff
            mirroring clouds in the mown-down

fields, spitting bird bones through the flesh of his teeth.

II

Poem in Three Voices

(Sappho, Catullus)

How many nights like a woman
in your woman's arms—how
many prone beneath moonlight—
the scent of lilacs over the
moist animal scent of ourselves?
Once there were days that shone
for us with rare brightness, O
tender girl picking flowers,
O sweet-voiced girl. Days
that shone with rare brightness.
Now this woman in your woman's
arms, a flower necklace at her throat;
her stature: precious, queenly.
How many nights her body
ghosted over mine in your slant
imaginings; how many nights
my own fragrant ghostings?
For me now, neither the honey
nor the bee, just this wasp
the color of charcoal, color of
smoke: how its madness
penetrates the very blue of the
glass. The windowsills—
a battlefield of domestic wreckage—
Achilles of the particled rain,
stung with dust; Brisêis in her
garments of bone-white silk,
happy that she's been stolen.
With whose eyes?
In mine she matches the gods,

that woman who sits there
facing you, but my tongue
breaks down saying these things
and then all at once a liquid fire
overwhelms my skin—dull,
wretched skin of the hands,
dull sheath of the body
turned inside out like a snakeskin
in moonlight. O the pessaries of
dough, red clay, grass, products
of the earth wedged against me:
day lily (crushed); columbine
(crushed); pale, fleshy hue
of the iris. This is what
the wasp says—*be all sting*—
its nest a harsh moon tucked
beneath the overhang,
soaked heavy with venom—fire-
flies lifting their delicate, banded
underbellies from the darkening grass.
"I was in love with you, Attis,
once long ago." That's what
she says, but what a woman
says to a passionate lover should be
scribbled on wind, on running
water. Now this scribbling
of wind, of running water,
this ritual eating of bark...
From a dream: I kept a bumblebee
named Molly, or Lucia, Lesbia,
I can't recall—*my veil, my wave,*
my wife—

To Keep Herself from Me

                                    the use of plugs and potions;
talismans on a leather cord
                        around her neck

(the poor crying child—not yet a child—
                                    adrift
in a universe of tears—*white blow*

                                    among the white-blown stars).
While down here, in blind rooms
                        and attic crawl spaces,

on islands in the middle of a city,
                        the middle
of the day, tufts of grass

                    and wool
to dam the cervix,
                sponges

soaked in oil and honey;
                    essence of alum, rock salt,
vinegar, soap;

            a cut lemon on the nightstand;
intricacies of tongue
                and hand…

And for my part, what?—oils of balsam
                                and cedar
to anoint the penis,

                    barriers of brightly-colored silk.
These things she ingested—
                              sap of pennyroyal

and Queen Anne's lace,
                    barrenwort,
birthwort;

          stalks of rue—
the nights
          when she chose to speak

(or did not speak)
              quick with it.
Now each heart packed with coagulated milk,

              concoctions of sugar and honey,
lard and honey—
              let it leach out

and extend the muscle—
                    the burn of it gone,
a painless debridement;

                    the pale animal
writhing of our bodies
                    spent

like moonlight onto the shattered ivory of the sheets.

Fragment

… abominable fascination: hate and
—love. The days (once)
all over us like melted jewel,
rare unguent. Then
twilight's bleed-through,
night's black ice. It is no mean feat,
this crawling.
It makes the knees *shine*.

Little Odysseus

Once, not so long ago, an uncle said

his favorite music was amphetamines

and heroin there beside the Chevy

red as my father's sister's lips

in Kodachrome beside the farm

that tender, idiot ghost walk

we all took among the livestock

then fled to the city, its siren song

summers cut like x-rays into the toes

my mother singing to vials of colored water

her little valiums, glycerins

and then the pot roast steaming

like a prophet's head

in a rawness of peeled garden

two of kind, three of a kind

what my father needed

belt so quickly whisked through the loops

it was a single thing

that astonished even him

hurt even him

world I whored for

his forgiveness: a weed we pulled

from the lawn so that later

I was cut loose, free, a grown man

smiling beside me inside the cinema

his haircut burning

like a hospital ceiling

this is not the worst of it, the doctor

said, tweezering the cancerous thing

from my neck, there will be more

the skin will speckle, tag and flare

the day I finally cut the strapping deeper in

hogs swung on hooks like sodden

coats inside the slaughterhouse

cattle stunned, electric to their bony forelegs

I tongued the overcooked meat

the carrots, the juices

and let my mother's singing lure me home

Amish Linen

Where does the question go that will render this sublime? In
   what part of the field
given to radiance—
                    fierce patterns of chicory,

day lily, mustard-colored blossoms—
          as pale and coarse
as Amish linen?

               Days I linger on the slow curves
to watch the wives and daughters
                      hang the laundry out.

Crisp, black, buttonless pants,
                   and then the women's blouses,
all loose and drying in the summer breeze.

As if at any moment two good fabrics
                   might lie one above the other
in a shimmering array

of sunlight and color and consciousness.
                    Or in twilight
muting the fabric,

          the sons and daughters
already paired off, racing—
             it's Saturday night—

jostling on the hard seats, the leather reins
tightly gathered (*the boys' hands*)—
                iron hooves

sparking concrete—
                    shoulder-to-shoulder;
hip-to hip;
        forearms grazing.

Their horses' bodies lost in all that harness, pell-mell, runaway.

III

Lion and Gin

I pet my father like some big cat a hunter has set on the ground,
though I am in Iowa now and not the Great Rift Valley
and what I sense as tent canvas flapping, thick with waterproofing,
is cheap cotton
choked with starch.
Still, he is a lion on the gurney.
I talk a little to make sure he's dead.
I have some memory of riding his shoulders
through the fragrant night. Three fish coiled in a creel. So many
butterflies
and gnats, it was two-thirds Kenya,
one-third Illinois.
And then home: the clink
of ice and gin.
And so I rub his hair, which is unwashed, and will
remain unwashed, for we will burn him.
I touch the blade of his chest.
Think of all those years I spent hovering beneath the scent of
Marlboros,
the mouthwash trace of booze; all that ice
cracking, going stale: crowned molars and mimic glaciers
fading to bled-out amber among the cuticles of lime.
Maybe that's why when he so blindly flies
on that exaltation of velocity and gas,
he doesn't linger in this world awhile as word or song,
a density we might gather round—
an aquifer, or gushing spring, as pure as gin.
Instead, he departs
as vapor.
Fragments of tooth and bone in the swept-out mass I can
throw back to dirt, or spread—a child's sugared, grainy drink—
to water.

And now I wonder, where's the soul in this?
The agent of it?
If it untags, retags itself—a flexible, moveable,
graffiti—indelible for the time we have it,
or if it sputters on some inward cycle toward a Rubbermaid
waste bucket, sink trap ringed with cocktail residue.
As on my returning, the trays of ice were reduced to spit.
I had a drink in my hand,
that memory of riding; the fragrant night.
How can I open the freezer now and not see the milky irises
of his passage;
the array of paw and pelt;
jaw wrenched so far open in that rictus of longing, gasping,
his living eyes could not help but tip and follow?

Whitman Burning

And then you were pulverized coral,

the process by which you
were rendered to ash beyond my Fahrenheit understanding as the
gauge clicked as if it were counting a swarm of maddened
bees—

a degree, it seemed, a second—

and the conveyor turned
and the whorled aluminum door closed down and those first
hot blasts—

a choir of tongues—enveloped the box.

How many
years you worked to fashion such corrugated structures—for
Coke and Pepsi, Maytag, the washers slipped in and dinged by
careless workmen, the cases shaken to their carbonated cores.

Now
men in lab coats are your deliverance. They had paperwork to
do but let me watch and so I paced as the hive of fire began its
honeyed work.

I put a poem of Whitman's there and waited as
it, too, rose in its mineral flash.

Two hours, they said, and then
a cool down from that white heat.

And then it was all in my
hands—the poem, the box and the blanket, the gold of your
teeth, my words inked across the face of Whitman.

I made
everybody touch you, the little baggie I had.

And then I drove to
the river.

Just up from Davenport, along the Mississippi, I found
a flat rock warmed by sun where I could sit and watch a barge
slug upstream, swooping gulls.

And then I heaved a handful.

Some
of you was spirited by wind and hissed as it took the current—
a gray-white alchemy I was not master of.

Some of you fell like
bone to the bottom.

I had to swish my hands a bit to drive you
deeper.

And then the barge passed, churning you up, the same,
or different gulls began their wheeling.

I felt better then—I
could drive home.

I knew nothing more than what I knew
before about misery or grief, the river of language, how it twists
and dazzles and, finally, does not matter,

even at 1600 degrees,
and it was a relief, actually, no burden,

though I wanted to utter
your bones—

by some last chemical process or blast of meta-
physics, Whitman's face pressed so close to the flaring heart
stem the aftershock was vision—

your bones your riven bones were
ruby, emerald.

Kiva Burning

MASTER
Daizui said, "Destroyed!"—what's it mean?
PUPIL
Saying, "Bari, bari, bari," the pupil flicks his hands,
giving the image of a blazing fire streaming in all
directions.

from *The Sound of the One Hand* (trans. Yoel Hoffman)

My hands are fire; their shadows
burn into the river, flicker
a swallow's width off magnetic north
until that cold quadrant falls
and a mourning dove
can haul it through in its heavy
winging. And then I turn them
east from where the river is
flowing, a brown thing rippling—
backwards, it seems—river grass
in shoals like tongues of fire. How
easily the current spills and burns
the length of the planet. A slow
fuse cutting three ways beneath
the concrete footings, em-
bracing the bridge and its traffic,
the rusted-out cars, battered
bike racks, the hospital west of
here where a friend's body
drifts eight stories up these
chill spring nights in a bower
of photographs and cotton, her blood
so crowded out it is spilling white,

the color of paste, the fats they
feed her, the color of moonlight.
There is a roundness there
(as there is here beside the river),
and a fevered burning.
Her eyes rolled up like my father's
eyes, the jaw lax in its sucking
for breath, as if the world
were not sustenance enough,
were not mercy enough,
and so they had to brick up
the windows, lay wood to walls,
fire to wood, and burn their
kivas, wander south. That day at
Chaco I sat a long time on the mesa's
lip before I climbed down into
the ghost coordinates—sun and
moon—and placed my hands
like fire along the equinoctial
bricks, stood above the burned-
out hollows. Saw
how where flame had touched them
the stones were scarred. And then
just as easily I was in the Diné
market, the secular aisles
another kind of holy place
where I could walk and become
one small thing inside
the ordinary and purchase jerky,
an avocado I thought to be ripe,
a jar of salsa, tin of chicken.
Where could I go then that would
not have me? This round place
burning in the desert. My
friend's face upturned to whatever

strictures of dust and light
will drop onto her from the ceiling.
My father's forehead still warm
minutes after we'd lost him
and so I bent down and put my lips
as if to the face of a brick, the skin
bruised red where the fire of
dying had touched him, the
mud-wash of living long fallen
to the ground, Pueblo Bonito,
dust on my boots, grit on my tongue,
being unable to speak finally,
and so just rubbing his hair, the
sweat and grease of it, rubbing
my own hair beside the ruins, a lizard
behind me balancing in sunlight on
footpads so precisely set into the dry
earth they might as well be seeds.

On *Purgatorio I*

Go with this man, see that you gird his waist
with a smooth reed; take care to bathe his face...

Sometimes mercy fell all the way down and made tiny windows in the fields. And sometimes it simply hovered in the seven times twenty panes of glass. It's not that I couldn't stand such utter selflessness—one thing passing into another across the distance—it's just that the sun resembled more a burning kite than star and stained the building with the pinks and muted oranges, muted yellows, of its raging sorrow. Still, it held me there winter sunset, and stood me helpless. The beauty was in the fuel of the thing. How each window banked like ignited water, the red bricks riffling in the perfect residue of seconds... Years later, it was my daughter wandering casually in to watch me bathing that undid me. How she played with the stacked towels awhile, toothpaste, soap, until this game bored her and she turned to me to wash my face and hair as only a child can: in the frank, religious spirit of cleansing, nursing. Awed, I let her scrub me. I let the grimed water sheet me like a radiant cloak until this too bored her and she wandered back to play with toys, left me chilled above the whirr of traffic. *I was in the car again.* It was 1968. The dream-time was all around me spilling the others' blood, the car that held us such a poor kite to the hill's wind. I remember waking upside down above the pivot and knowing nothing of time but a kind of hurry-up to save the cell-life, my father's borrowed jacket on another scrunched beside me in the filtering light... *Witless*, our ritual cleansings, the actual timings: a second window flared beneath me on the bitter earth. I dropped and hurried toward it, crawled hands and knees into the charity and utter coarseness that was ditch grass.

(False) Ambient

(above the dam)

What I hear upstream
from the power plant is a
three-part cabling of

engine and falling
liquid through the run of pipes;
steam: gray-blue, gray-pink

plumage pouring from
the towers. Though some of it
(sense of this turbine

running through me, this
spirit, bird) will fracture to
rain and re-enter

the cycle—a drift
of prayer rags, incense—what
this attention comes

down to, this body
of dreaming, now my shadow
is marring the riv-

er, and flares like a
post on fire; haloes and smol-
ders…

　　　*

(below the dam)

      Gates closed, the
river is merely whistle
now, pinched runoff

and easy sidlings.
The twenty miles above me,
behind me—a sway-

ing roof, glacial,
kinetic. Here, islands pro-
trude, and shoals of rock,

in a churning af-
terlife. A heron wings in
like a broken kite

as blue as sunrise.
Sidewalks, rocks: flat, reflective;
heated surface. All

around me the vis-
ible in a drying swirl.
The hillside still strung

with morning's backwash—
banked in this sprung world like a
dulcimer. The riv-

er on its fulcrum:
a scale for dog-yelp, dog-bark,
fish line, down—

     ✳

(coda: coal pile)

        At the
end of this world, this city
block, it is perhaps

one diamond strong
the pile of coal that feeds us.
An obsidian

whale laid out in a
stretch of fin and heaving, breath
sucked in and pressed

to its house of ribs—
the long, narrowing dive for
the infinites-

imal, animal
krill; clouds and swarms, metric tons
of them sheened to in-

sight in the inky
depths, the small cries collapsing,
sense of my own mind

collapsing, becoming
this one thing, baleens gushing
(coal pocketed on

a fretted slide toward
the furnace's oil-fed blasts), could
I set my listen-

ing—and the heart's path,
heart's intention—now *just so*
inside the facet.

IV

Viewing the Holy Ghost, Horseshoe Canyon

Then, suddenly, this body: all ochre,
                    ground hematite,
          adrift on a rock

expanse: a spiritual,
                    precise graffiti,
          the face of god thrown,

finally, in the name of mud
                    (the binding agent:
          organic, unknown),

some of it painted, pecked;
                    some of it
          dribbled and left to run

(snake in real time,
                    a desert bull,
          sliding its black-braided water

through dust and grass,
                    my body laid,
          sacrificial, on a heated stone).

I could hear it stop—the snake—
                    sift again
          the coarseness—

aridness etched; each serrated blade
                    of time—
          some of me blown

like mist from the mouth—
            exploding star,
        all paint and spittle. Dimensionality

(sweat streaking an upper check)
            like a sect mark,
        the way the Holy Ghost is marked,

was marked (our name/
            their image)
        2000 B.C.E. And so he strides,

Barrier Canyon Style,
            out of sheered flatness
        into a pool of shade—

an armless, legless spirit prowling
            the threshold.
        Iterations of the kinetic,

the sacred. So that hiking out
            of the canyon
        even the ravens were part of it—

one crying black streaks
            into that penetrable,
        massive silence;

stalling in effortless down-swoop
            before a gap
        in the rock;

then swift, cursive upleap—
            wings
        spread—wings dampened…

balance at the nest's lip.
The other raven
shrieking. Taking mouth

from mouth—raven kiss,
raven breath,
twig bit; a weight-

lessness: desert silk. Because
who
wouldn't want, in the end,

the unlikeness to roll away, and
the artistry
arise: goat, god, sheep; human, human.

Catfish

The river, too, was unscaled,
undulate,
fin and muscle

moving over fin and muscle,
day's sludge
and night's marl

falling in sheets
of shit
and mica,

farm runoff leaching its
penetrant sorghum
so the artery

we loved was sugared,
poisoned.
Still, the water

yielded. We fished
from the bridge,
hauling

the bodies up
like drunks
from the eddies,

then nailing them
hard fast to planks we had set
against a rotting shed,

ripping
with our daddy's pliers
their kimono silks.

Wind throbbed in the
lilacs; the sound
of their tearing

—the transformation
complete,
all that primal mud

and excess fluoride,
the city's
contaminants, rendered

on the tongue
to lemon's sting, petals
of succulent meat.

And then the albino,
white of
an egg, crushed chalk

of moon.
And then their bones
driven deep in the garden.

Crazy Horse Mountain

Uprootedness is what I wanted—out of the ground
        of my skin
    a fierce yanking—

so that later I was disappointed at first,
        and then
    reluctantly blessed, when the Sioux warrior,

counting coup, tapped my arm
        for Jesus. Christ,
    how I'd spent years dodging

that chrome icon, my sins in his fist,
        my body
    elsewhere: a vine twisting along a rusty nail.

And so I thought: whose God then?
        Whose spirit
    driven like a pony before the wind?

It was all play, of course—*I am*
        quicker than you, braver—
    but still, I wanted

to leap up and strike him back, wave
        the ceremonial wing—
    a violation?—

like healing smoke

※

toward holiness…

And so I ate the fry bread, tuned in
            to Hank Williams
      all morning,

stood before the quartz stalks
            of Crazy Horse's eyes
      (who was never photographed)

and let myself be stolen—
            Nikon, Pentax;
      digital, video—

my flesh spirit mixed with stone spirit
            dynamited
      from rock

taken in strands like spider's silk,
            or braided rope—
      a crash

                    ✳

            and reckless fountaining…

O Shirtwearer, Curly, Light Hair,
            His Horse Stands in Sight,

where is that warrior now,
            the one you dreamed,
      who took no scalps,

spoke little, dressed plainly,
            zigzag lightning
      marking his cheek,

hail dotting the body, rider shaken so fiercely
his loose hair
was the wing of a hawk…

Just now, the moon

＊

has let fly its glass horse
over the Dakotas,

filling the campsite with arctic light,
though the air
is 90, and the tent

is folding like my mind
with the wind.
Sometimes lying down so flat

it shimmers—like a mirage, or water.
Sometimes swelling like a lung.
I'll have to weigh

its weathered fabric with two or three
heavy stones—
to anchor sleep—

or wait until the stars come out,
trickster-flung,
and let their milky wash recast me.

Deer, Crows

When you scraped the deer's hairs from the rear-
                    view mirror
          and buried them in the yard,

sending words into the earth with them, I ran
                    my hand along
          its body's shape thrown

into sheet metal: here, where the shoulder
                    came in
          straight and made a bowl; there,

where its body flipped and its rump grazed
                    the rear quarter
          panel. The shape of its spirit, maybe,

made heavy by speed, the angle of its
                    crossing
          against velocity. A second deer

had already leapt through, invisible
                    inside our
          vision, its white tail flicking

beyond the interstate. And then that cartwheel
                    tumbling of the
          other, as if it were our own bodies

outside the car, leaning in, breaking,
                    though you
          choked the steering and braked hard,

and the tonnage of us veered. Such a compact
glide into panic,
the traffic pulled by on tethers

of light, honking as the animal staggered,
or at the pace
of your weeping, flopped wildly

on bleeding haunches. When we drove
the same road
back, days later, in stunning daylight,

we looked into the tawny, too-high shoulder
grass for
the nest of its presence. Then, seeing

nothing, looked for crows…
I know this is wrong
but I test them when I drive,

slowing down to disrupt their gyros,
then speeding
up, as if I could crash that moment

when the pressure shifts and they
ungainly lift,
flap some deer's body length away.

Stalk back over after my car has passed
to jab again,
and tear and feed. I think blood still

shines on them, makes them even blacker,
slicker. I think
their morning cries still wake me,

freighting some spirit-shred onto
               the next county road,
          lapsed pasture. Mid-autumn sunset,

I worry the interstate with too much
               speed—to pick
          you up—a vector of

luck, cage of flesh, hammered metal.
               And then
          beyond the crushed stones, spray

of diamonds—one doe in goatsbeard,
               quietly feeding.
          I slow or speed—it doesn't matter.

Some raw physics bleeds with nightfall,
               the deer's
          exhalation (my car raging forward)

wetting the grass stalks—a smear of
               phlegm
          and its astonishment—flashing through

this sinking world as weightless as a sparrow.

Tarkovsky's Horse

Andrei Rublev

Not the one saved from the slaughterhouse for this.
> Gunshot
>> to the chest just before the camera rolls

so the full thousand pounds of it
>> can stumble down the staircase.
> Like boiling metal poured

down a throat except it is the heart that fountains.
>> A jet or spray
> as thin as water,

Rublev, painter of icons,
>> on his knees elsewhere,
> until the animal staggers stiff-legged

in the blindness that is death.
>> Rocks on its haunches.
> Rears. *Deus equus*.

Takes a spear like mercy to the chest. No,
>> not this horse.
> But the other.

The one from the prologue—
>> the animal
> on its back, its fine muscular volume

working the dust into its glistening coat,
>> before it rolls
> back over,

wholly alive. Kneels in that posture
            that in Rublev
      is spirit driven down into the wicker

of the hands, the little spits that atomize
            his pleading, but
      that in the horse is instinctual grace. Bounces

once, hooves flashing. Canters away.
            For it is the animals
      in the film we follow,

the metal—dual nature—
            flesh and
      sky of them, the Tartars running

their fast ponies before the burning city,
            peeling gold
      from the cathedral towers

as geese fly. Or earlier, the slaughter of swans.
            The holy fool
      in a circle

of dogs. And then that living horse,
            which is not Rublev,
      but liquid earth rising,

and then, later, a boy,
            a cooling stream
      of it, who driven past virus

and hunger, lies. Says he can fashion
            bells.
      The prince's men are looking for his father,

a maker of bells. But the father is dead—
                    and so the boy
          lies. Follows them back to the city,

says this is the creative
                    spirit, raw earth, clay.
          Digs it out in rain

to daub a giant cast. And the townsfolk
                    believe him—
          render over

knives and forks, cups and plates
                    to the fires he builds
          to feed the hollowness

its honey. For it is like a hive
                    Rublev wanders
          around—a wet dog—through the ruts

of his faith, edge of the story,
                    not painting,
          watching the boy.

Rublev has killed, has set his robes on fire,
                    let the boat
          of paganism softly knock

his own wooden craft packed with monks.
                    Then silence,
          listless gazing. So when they

haul it up—the bell—like the very
                    weight of
          earth itself and lay the hammer

on, it is as if from inside himself
        he hears
    it peal—like faith, a lie, belief…

The boy falls to the mud, crying. Rublev,
        too,
    for they are now one thing

kneeling in birth matter, clapper
        and lip,
    hammer and rope, air and mud.

Rublev will paint; the boy forge bells.
        There is Christ
    now in it… It rings. It is sweet, and it rings.

V

Kurosawa's Dog

Even though he's dead, my father dreams repeatedly
                  of the Eisenhower era.
        The clarity of fresh concrete spanning the Great Plains.

That runway-hill-runway slow curve north or south rhythm
                  across the face of my childhood.
        His fatherhood.

My own memory is of a helicopter flying over our house
                  through the sorghum haze
        drifting from the Quaker Oats plant on the south side.

What I remember is the smell and the gleam.
                  My father pointing
        to a dot in the sky as bald as Khrushchev, saying, "Look."

I am considering buying a gun. I suspect this is the result of my
                  father's dying.
        I know his anger fuels it. Anger at his father for giving away

the farm or stealing the hog he raised on kitchen scraps.
                  Anger at his mother
        and her rattlesnake of braids.

The Navy tattoo stinging where he razored it off.
                  I want the crispness of the shot, the recoil,
        the settling in again on the target.

And those years, 1956 into the early sixties.
                  My tumbling towheaded with a busted lip
        along the river bank while he hauled up catfish or carp

the size of my arms, and knocked back beers.
                    And those slow, sad trips through towns with
          Indian names to the farm. Once

(I am remembering this, I am already haunting my waking life),
                    he and I were feeding chickens
          just before his father died. It was Sunday

and he was still wearing his pressed Sunday shirt so when the sun
                    angled through and hit him,
          he disappeared above his pants.

From torso and target, to nothingness. As clear as albumen.
                    Now each bullet (imaginary) smacks the
          membrane of paper and leaves a finger-sized hole in the skin

of his rage. I have questions. Is it better there than here?
                    Yes, I'm okay, don't worry.
          Have you seen God?

No, but my brother is here, and my mother. Have you stopped
                    drinking?
          And then from nowhere, that smell as if from the inside

of his hat. An aura of flesh and grease, cultured by wool and heat.
                    An earth smell, water smell.
          Grief rolling its head and mumbling the tone poem

of the dead. When I buried my father, it was like setting a book
                    in the earth. A box
          like a composite of ash, or scabbed-over skin.

A man (a gardener, I think) met me at the mausoleum.
                    He had a hook in his hand, a shovel,
          the book of ashes.

There was a manhole cover under a bed of ornamental stones.
                    The man shoveled the stones aside,
            hooked the cover open, set the book on top of other books

in the fake lump of hillside. There was a wall of names
                            and dates but nothing corresponded.
            My father was not a letter addressed to God.

More like the top book in a stack of books next to God's unmade
                    bed. Something from His to-read list.
            Some ash fiction.

What is time but a slow worm eating its way through our lives.
                    A slow bullet with a glistening afterwash
            we call memory or loss.

Khrushchev arguing with Nixon over kitchen appliances.
                    Francis Gary Powers,
            a black spirit falling from the sky.

My father's one and only love perfecting the casserole.
                    And then one day, when I am doing dishes,
            I know I have lost him.

He will not return. I wonder if I have offended him,
                    loved him too much,
            not enough.

Relished in his sins, which were many, too readily.
                    My own, which are partially his.
            Where does rage go after we die?

Is it picked up like a flu or virus? A temporary haze.
                    Or does it cut through whoever remains
            like a back pasture creek bed.

Dusk moves like gold paint over everything. Clouds shift. Trees
spring and collapse.
I dream I am Kurosawa's dog.

I trot with a severed hand in my mouth.
It's that moment in *Yojimbo,* a film from 1961,
the Eisenhower years.

I wonder: Did Ike see it? Did Nixon? Did that helicopter
ever land in our town
where we were never really happy, but always poor?

It is okay at first—this feeling—because I am trotting
and somebody—not me—
is staggering backwards.

My father as Toshiro Mifune, or God, Eisenhower, as Toshiro
Mifune, trapped
between some self-serving clan of alcohol and rice.

Another—like their shirts—of silk.
Landscape reduced
(it will become our fear) to smoke and ash. And then it is my

own hand in my mouth—I am biting the hand—cooling me down.

Does Not Sleep

My father has pulled this fish out of me. A northern pike
he lays on a bed of ice in a bathtub, Minnesota, 1958,
so I am up all night slapping my hands in the wet,
saying, *you little son of a bitch*, and letting its cold flanks
say back to me *the rouged cheek* or *the bare asses of
waves*, so that the beating (along the shore) is already
built into the shape, and the waves in that part of night
are lullaby. Both parent and child grow groggy, sleep.
But the fish does not sleep. It is a child buried
in a snowbank, a white tunnel collapsed. Somebody
has dug all night to find this body, this meat —a
tremor of muscle, its lips pulled back, teeth bared.

Deer Poem

So now the placement of the "I" to the edge of this field: two
    deer running.
Night's chilled touch—skin of the air upon
                              the skin of their hides,

all that darting and stepping through high grass, the worn trails
flooding with starlight.
                Bird song, cricket trill;

the tongue flaring in their singular mind—*such coarse whistling*—;
the heart muscling up like a leopard—they sense
                my presence—
                      prelude to flight.

The deer's souls (if they possess souls) no more now than
    blood feathers
in nothing's song—flash of a sparrow drenched
with rain; or hawk

            cry, owl cry; a flock of crows
so stretched along the gray horizon, it is one bird and then one
    bird,
an isolated cry,

echoes ringing to the bleached skull of moon. Clouds stall, linger
in darkness
        above this other darkness;

the cool, elegant ropes of spine uncoil. Bodies collapse. Nests of
    grass
flatten and pool, settle and pool—
                purr of

the river past uncut fields pressed so deep into the night it is the
    earth itself.

Resurrection Yoga

New skin, new skin—a spotted lizard now, my father wriggles and thrives. And all that time I thought he was a man. But desert prefers him. All that baked air swelling his lungs which were too moist, living, too much like wet sacks weighing him down. And so rocks prefer him. Desert blossoms light his passage. I saw him once, that time at Arches. It was evening, a last stroll, light falling in long, gold sheets, and there he scooted, vogued, and scooted, kicking up clouds of sand like cigarette puffs. I knew it was him by how he breathed, hard-pressed in the heat. Step, and intake, gasp and intake. I thought: even the floor of heaven must scorch. I had no water to give him, and so I just stood, like him, bare-skinned, rounded, balancing on my left foot awhile (*whisper* of sand the wind scythed through). Then settling hard with my right.

Coyote Bliss

High summer, interstate: in the mile after I'd dropped
               you off, there
        was a body, one of God's dogs,

at the road's side, contradictory and ambiguous,
               its gross physical
        sheathing about to burst through

its sheath of intelligence,
               whatever was left
        of it, its sheath of bliss.

Still the animal held its carriage,
               skin and body,
        bone, so much a part of the landscape

I cannot think without it: paws
               held rigid
        as if to repel the sun: song fragments,

fragments of its trace,
               from restlessness to abiding,
        its last pained yip, hurt howl.

Elsewhere, once,
               I bent
        to touch another's left forepaw ridged

in mud, New Mexico desert, off-trail
               creek bed,
        mustard-yellow stone chalked

so perfectly into the surrounding hillsides
                    it was a remnant
          of wind, wind's upswept tail.

Some sovereign mineral whispering
                    to the form
          I was, and nudging. And so I let it nudge.

I dreamed blue fire, ghost of water,
                    paw print,
          coyote saving the bones for O'Keeffe

(O'Keeffe painting the bones), the fragments
                    resting upon,
          the clouds between fragments

until the wind picked up
                    and was stone
          again, and I shook myself dusty

in its thrashing. Looked for snakes. Thought
                    again of that other
          rabid creature I walked twice past

on the Canyon's south rim as if
                    to ruin
          my life, to fuck it up, fuck it royally,

chaos soaking me in saffron, coyote
                    (seen by the eyes
          of God) working the scrub…

On the flight back: storm front, a hundred or so
                    miles of it,
          lightning breaking like glass at 20,000 degrees

in a living animal's eye, forest line
            down below
      exploding with dusk, whole acres ripped

to fiery plumes, though I could not
            hear them
      above the engine's constant mechanical

whirr—inside my head like a wind,
            like a trail,
      like a scent... I thought: I, too, shall fly

home. I shall eat well (eat anything), sing planet on fire.

Notes

"Bresson's Donkey": *Au Hasard, Balthazar* (1966), directed by Robert Bresson. The italicized lines are from *The Odyssey*, translated by Robert Fitzgerald.

"On a Watch Chain Woven from Hair, Dated 23.10.22": For my father's mother.

"*Cruel All Moons and Bitter the Suns*": The title and quoted/echoed passages are from *The Drunken Boat*, translated by Louise Varèse. Some of the detail in this poem was gathered from *Paleoecological Interpretation of the Late Quaternary Wapsipinicon Local Fauna (Empty Fissure and Dutch Creek Fissure Local Faunules), Jones County, Iowa*, Principal Investigator: Steven Wallace.

"Poem in Three Voices": Texts that provided material for this poem are: *Catullus*, translated by Peter Whigham; *Catullus*, translated by Charles Martin; *Sappho*, translated by Mary Barnard; *Sappho*, translated by Jim Powell.

"To Keep Herself from Me": Some of the detail in this poem was gathered from *Honey, Mud, Maggots and Other Medical Marvels: The Science Behind Folk Remedies and Old Wives' Tales*, by Robert and Michele Root-Bernstein.

"Fragment": *Catullus*, translated by Charles Martin.

"On *Purgatorio I*": Epigraph translated by Mark Musa. For my daughter.

"Catfish": For Dennis McMillan, for the silk and pliers.

"Deer, Crows": For Teresa Schulz.

"Tarkovsky's Horse": *Andrei Rublev* (1969), directed by Andrei Tarkovsky.

"Kurosawa's Dog": *Yojimbo* (1961), directed by Akira Kurosawa.

"Coyote Bliss": Some of the detail in this poem was gathered from a piece on Georgia O'Keeffe by Terry Tempest Williams. For Gerry LaFemina.

Acknowledgments

Grateful acknowledgment to the editors of the magazines in which the following poems (or earlier versions) first appeared:

The Adirondack Review: "Lion and Gin"; *The Alaska Quarterly*: "Amish Linen"; *American Literary Review*: "On *Purgatorio I*"; *Black Warrior Review*: "Fragment"; *Crab Orchard Review*: "*Cruel All Moons and Bitter the Suns*"; *FIELD*: "Does Not Sleep" and "Kurosawa's Dog"; *Hunger Mountain*: "(False) Ambient" and "Kiva Burning"; *Natural Bridge*: "Deer Poem"; *Paradidomi Review*: "Catfish" and "Portrait of My Father as the Heather Vole"; *Redivider*: "Little Odysseus"; *Sou'wester*: "Coyote Bliss," "Deer, Crows," and "Resurrection Yoga"; *Terminus*: "Whitman Burning"; *Third Coast:* "Crazy Horse Mountain"; *Willow Springs*: "The Sound-of-One-Hand-Clapping Shout."

"Poem in Three Voices" and "To Keep Herself from Me" first appeared in *Notre Dame Review* #23, Winter 2007.

"Tarkovsky's Horse" first appeared in *Notre Dame Review* #27, Winter 2009.

"Viewing the Holy Ghost, Horseshoe Canyon" first appeared in *Evensong: Contemporary American Poets on Spirituality*, published by Bottom Dog Press.

"Coyote Bliss" and "Crazy Horse Mountain" also appeared in *Evensong: Contemporary American Poets on Spirituality*, published by Bottom Dog Press.

"Amish Linen," "On *Purgatorio I*," and "The Sound-of-One-Hand-Clapping Shout" (as "Zen Shout") also appeared in the limited edition chapbook *Message to Be Spoken into the Left Ear of God*, published by Mayapple Press. Thanks to Judith Kerman.

A shout across the rooftops to the following individuals for camaraderie, friendship, and feedback as I worked on these poems: Laura Apol, Suzanne Berger, Jay Featherstone, Chuck Fleck, Gerry LaFemina, Dawn Newton, John Pijewski, Michael Ripple, Leonora Smith, Ruelaine Stokes, and Dick Thomas.

Thanks also to David Young, David Walker, and everyone at Oberlin College Press.